STRUCTURAL WONDERS

COLOSSEUM

by Kelsey Jopp

FOCUS READERS

READERS

NAVIGATOR

WWW.FOCUSREADERS.COM

Focus Readers is distributed by North Star Editions:
sales@northstareditions.com | 888-417-0195

Produced for Focus Readers by Red Line Editorial.

Photographs ©: Shutterstock Images, cover, 1, 4–5, 7, 9, 13, 19, 23, 27, 29; Hubert Robert/Album/Oronoz/Newscom, 10–11; José Antonio Peñas/Science Source, 15; North Wind Picture Archives/Alamy, 16–17; Lordprice Collection/Alamy, 21; Album/Prisma/Newscom, 24–25

Library of Congress Cataloging-in-Publication Data
Names: Jopp, Kelsey, 1993- author.
Title: Colosseum / by Kelsey Jopp.
Description: Lake Elmo, MN : Focus Readers, [2023] | Series: [Structural wonders] | Includes index. | Audience: Grades 4-6
Identifiers: LCCN 2022026205 (print) | LCCN 2022026206 (ebook) | ISBN 9781637394786 (hardcover) | ISBN 9781637395158 (paperback) | ISBN 9781637395844 (pdf) | ISBN 9781637395523 (ebook)
Subjects: LCSH: Colosseum (Rome, Italy)--Juvenile literature. | Amphitheaters--Rome--Juvenile literature. | Rome (Italy)--Buildings, structures, etc.--Juvenile literature. | Architecture, Roman--Italy--Rome--Juvenile literature.
Classification: LCC DG68.1 .J67 2023 (print) | LCC DG68.1 (ebook) | DDC 937/.63--dc23/eng/20220608
LC record available at https://lccn.loc.gov/2022026205
LC ebook record available at https://lccn.loc.gov/2022026206

Printed in the United States of America
Mankato, MN
012023

ABOUT THE AUTHOR
Kelsey Jopp is an editor, writer, and lifelong learner. She lives in Minnesota, where she enjoys swimming in lakes and playing endless fetch with her sheltie, Teddy.

TABLE OF CONTENTS

CHAPTER 1

A Symbol of Rome 5

CHAPTER 2

A Gift to the People 11

CHAPTER 3

Deadly Games 17

THAT'S AMAZING!

Beneath the Colosseum 22

CHAPTER 4

The Colosseum Today 25

Focus on the Colosseum • 30
Glossary • 31
To Learn More • 32
Index • 32

A SYMBOL OF ROME

Sturdy stone columns line a walkway. Above, the stones curve into a series of impressive arches. At the end of the walkway, sunlight pours through an entrance. The space opens into a vast arena. Nearly 2,000 years ago, **gladiators** stood here. They prepared for a fight to the death. Today, tourists walk about.

The Colosseum is one of the most popular tourist sites in Europe.

5

They learn about the history of this ancient space.

The Roman Colosseum is a huge amphitheater. An amphitheater is a large open area surrounded by seating. In ancient Rome, crowds filled the seats to be entertained. The Colosseum stands in the center of Rome, the capital city of Italy. The Roman Forum is also nearby. This plaza was where ancient Romans shopped for goods. **Ruins** of government buildings and churches surround the Forum.

The Colosseum was built in the first century CE. Emperor Vespasian ordered its construction. After he died, his

The ruins of the Roman Forum are a short walk from the Colosseum.

oldest son completed the structure. Then, Vespasian's other son added new features. These three emperors made up the Flavian dynasty. For this reason, the Colosseum is also known as the Flavian Amphitheater. But its more popular name comes from the word *colossal*. This term means "very large."

The Colosseum is very large, indeed. In ancient times, it measured 620 by 512 feet (189 by 156 m). Its four stories towered 150 feet (46 m) high. Large crowds came and went through 80 entrances. When filled, the Colosseum held 50,000 people. Today, it is the

ONE OF MANY

The Colosseum was not the only one of its kind. The Roman Empire was home to up to 400 amphitheaters. Many of these structures have not survived. Others still exist but are in ruins. However, four ancient amphitheaters are still in use today. People go to them to watch concerts and plays.

A tourist walks through the halls of the Colosseum.

largest ancient amphitheater still standing. It is also one of the New Seven Wonders of the World. These are famous structures from around the world. Visitors come from near and far to marvel at the Colosseum. For centuries, it has been a famous symbol of Rome.

CHAPTER 2

A GIFT TO THE PEOPLE

Before the Colosseum was built, Rome went through many difficult years. Emperor Nero was known for being cruel. He killed people for their religious beliefs.

The Great Fire of Rome took place during Nero's reign. This fire destroyed much of the city in 64 CE. After the fire, Nero built a palace for himself. It was

The Great Fire of Rome burned down approximately two-thirds of the city.

called the Golden House. It had fancy gardens and its own lake.

When Nero died, the Roman Empire elected a new leader. But none of the new emperors lasted long. In one year, Rome went through four emperors. Only the fourth, Vespasian, was successful.

Vespasian wanted to **restore** Rome. He also wanted to give a gift to the city's people. So, he called for the Colosseum to be built. He chose the area of the Golden House for construction. The Colosseum was built where Nero's lake used to be. The lake was drained. Then it was filled with concrete. This would help protect the structure against earthquakes.

Vespasian led Rome for 10 years, from 69 to 79 CE.

Construction on the Colosseum began in 72 CE. Most of the work was done by enslaved Jews. The Roman Empire had taken them prisoner during wars. More than 60,000 enslaved Jews worked on the Colosseum.

The Colosseum required huge amounts of planning. The structure had to be strong. So, it was made of stone and cement. Iron clamps held the blocks together. The building also featured many arches and columns. The spaces under the arches were filled with statues of emperors and gods.

The arena floor was made of wood. Then it was covered with sand. This was where gladiators would fight. As an amphitheater, the building had no roof. But it did have an awning. This fabric hung over part of the seating area. It provided shade to approximately one-third of the audience.

The amphitheater was finally finished in 80 CE. By this time, Vespasian had died. His son Titus took over. Titus celebrated the opening of the Colosseum with 100 days of games.

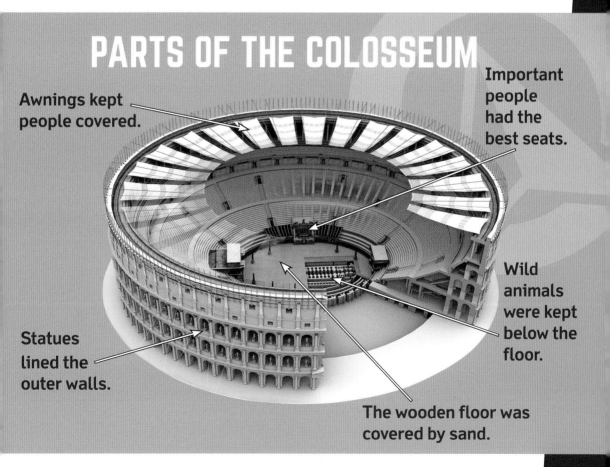

PARTS OF THE COLOSSEUM

Awnings kept people covered.

Important people had the best seats.

Wild animals were kept below the floor.

Statues lined the outer walls.

The wooden floor was covered by sand.

CHAPTER 3

DEADLY GAMES

The events that took place in the Colosseum were extremely violent. Some people fought one another to the death. Others fought wild animals. Even public **executions** took place. Over the years, approximately 400,000 people died in the Colosseum. More than one million animals also died.

Some people fought lions at the Colosseum.

Rome is well known for its gladiators. Most gladiators were forced to fight. Some were people who had been enslaved. Others had committed crimes. Over time, some gladiators volunteered to fight. They wanted to become famous. However, being a gladiator was not easy. First, people had to go to gladiator school. Here, masters taught them how to fight. Students had to give away their rights. Their masters controlled them. Most gladiators did not live long.

There were various types of gladiators. The *murmillo* wore heavy armor. They fought with swords and shields. The *retiarius* wore light armor. They trapped

A victorious gladiator could choose to spare his opponent's life.

their opponents with nets. Then they stabbed their rivals with spears. Another type was the *essedarius*. These gladiators fought on chariots. These carts were pulled by horses.

Meanwhile, the huge audience watched. Seating was very crowded. It was divided by social status. The emperor had the best seat. He sat closest to the action. He even had his own entrance. Near the emperor sat the nobles. These were powerful, wealthy people. Women and people without much money had the worst seats. They sat near the top.

FLOODING THE COLOSSEUM

Famous naval battles were sometimes recreated in the Colosseum. For these events, the arena's floor was flooded with water. Then dozens of boats entered. These boats were built specifically for the show. They had flat bottoms. That way, they did not scrape the floor. Gladiators on the boats acted out the battle. Afterward, the water was drained. Audiences left the Colosseum amazed.

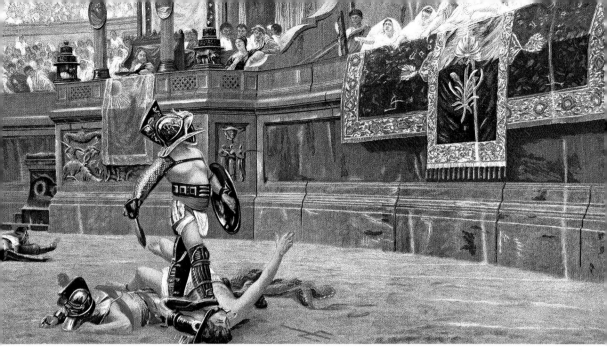

Members of the crowd used thumb signals to show whether they thought a gladiator should kill his opponent.

The games changed over the years. Training gladiators was costly, and gladiators died often. So, the empire made the games less deadly. Gladiators were taught to hurt their opponents without killing them. Other times, officials stopped the fights early. This allowed gladiators to fight again.

BENEATH THE COLOSSEUM

The Colosseum was known for its huge floor. That is where the fighting took place. But underneath the floor was the hypogeum. For years, this underground area was a mystery. By the 1800s, it was covered by 40 feet (12 m) of earth. In the 1900s, workers cleared it out.

A long stairway led down into the ruins. Weeds grew out of the stone walls. Both the walls and floors had deep grooves. These grooves once held lifts. During shows, animals were put onto the lifts. Next, the lifts were raised with a **winch**. The animals then appeared in the arena through trapdoors. To the audience, it seemed like magic. One lift could hold approximately 600 pounds (270 kg). That is the weight of two lions.

Today, the Colosseum has a modern reconstruction of a lift and trapdoor.

CHAPTER 4

THE COLOSSEUM TODAY

Over time, people became less interested in the games at the Colosseum. Rome was also going through changes. In 395 CE, the Roman Empire split in half. The Western Empire, which included the city of Rome, was weak. Its **economy** struggled. In 410, invaders took over Rome. By 476, the Western

In 410 CE, Visigoth invaders destroyed many buildings and stole goods from Roman citizens.

Empire had fallen. Romans were no longer in power.

In the years that followed, the Colosseum served other purposes. Sometimes it held religious ceremonies. At one point, it was a factory. At another point, it was a **fortress**. For years, it was

THE EARTHQUAKE OF 1349

The Colosseum was built to last. But over time, it became weaker. One reason was that people stole the metal clamps that held the stones together. Then, in 1349, a massive earthquake hit Rome. It destroyed most of the city. The earthquake shook the Colosseum. The outer south side of the building collapsed.

Many parts of the Colosseum have crumbled over the years.

not used at all. No one took care of it. People even carried away many of its stones to use as building materials.

Today, the Colosseum looks very different than it did in ancient times. Only one-third of the structure remains. Some of it was ruined by **vandalism**. Other parts were damaged by earthquakes and fires. Originally, the stone was covered in marble. But today, much of the Colosseum is bare.

Millions of people visit the Colosseum each year. However, tourism has its costs. Some people break the rules. They vandalize the Colosseum. Tourism also increases pollution. Dirty air harms the structure's ancient stones.

Many people have worked to protect the Colosseum. In the 1700s, taking materials from it became illegal. In the 1800s, workers began restoring parts of it. And in the late 1900s, major repair projects took place.

Tourists can get an excellent view of the area below the Colosseum's floor.

Today, the city of Rome is trying to improve the experience of tourists. For instance, people can now explore the hypogeum. Nearly 2,000 years have passed since the Colosseum was first built. But visitors still experience the awe of this structural wonder.

FOCUS ON
THE COLOSSEUM

Write your answers on a separate piece of paper.

1. Write a sentence that describes the main ideas from Chapter 3.

2. Do you think people have done enough to protect the Colosseum? Why or why not?

3. Which emperor ordered the Colosseum to be built?

> **A.** Nero
> **B.** Vespasian
> **C.** Titus

4. What happened to the marble that used to cover the Colosseum?

> **A.** It was destroyed by weather or stolen.
> **B.** It was used by gladiators during fights.
> **C.** It was covered up with other materials.

Answer key on page 32.

GLOSSARY

economy
A system of goods, services, money, and jobs.

executions
Acts of punishment in which people are killed.

fortress
A large, strong building that can be defended from attack.

gladiators
People who fought animals or other people for entertainment in ancient Rome.

restore
To return something to its original condition.

ruins
Broken pieces of buildings, especially ones from very long ago.

vandalism
Damage that is done to a building on purpose and without permission.

winch
A piece of equipment used for pulling and hauling heavy items.

TO LEARN MORE

BOOKS

Alkire, Jessie. *Exploring Ancient Cities*. Minneapolis: Abdo Publishing, 2019.

Bell, Samantha S. *Ancient Rome*. Lake Elmo, MN: Focus Readers, 2020.

Waxman, Laura Hamilton. *Mysteries of Pompeii*. Minneapolis: Lerner Publications, 2018.

NOTE TO EDUCATORS

Visit **www.focusreaders.com** to find lesson plans, activities, links, and other resources related to this title.

INDEX

animals, 17, 22

chariots, 19

earthquake, 12, 26, 28
executions, 17

flooding, 20
floor, 14, 20, 22

gladiators, 5, 14, 18–21

Golden House, 11–12

hypogeum, 22, 29

invaders, 25

Jews, 13

Nero, 11–12

Titus, 15
tourism, 28–29
trapdoors, 22

vandalism, 27–28
Vespasian, 6–7, 12, 15

Answer Key: 1. Answers will vary; **2.** Answers will vary; **3.** B; **4.** A